THE THIRTEEN COLONIES IN THE US:
3RD GRADE US HISTORY SERIES

The Thirteen Colonies were British colonies on the east coast of North America which had been founded between 1607 and 1732.

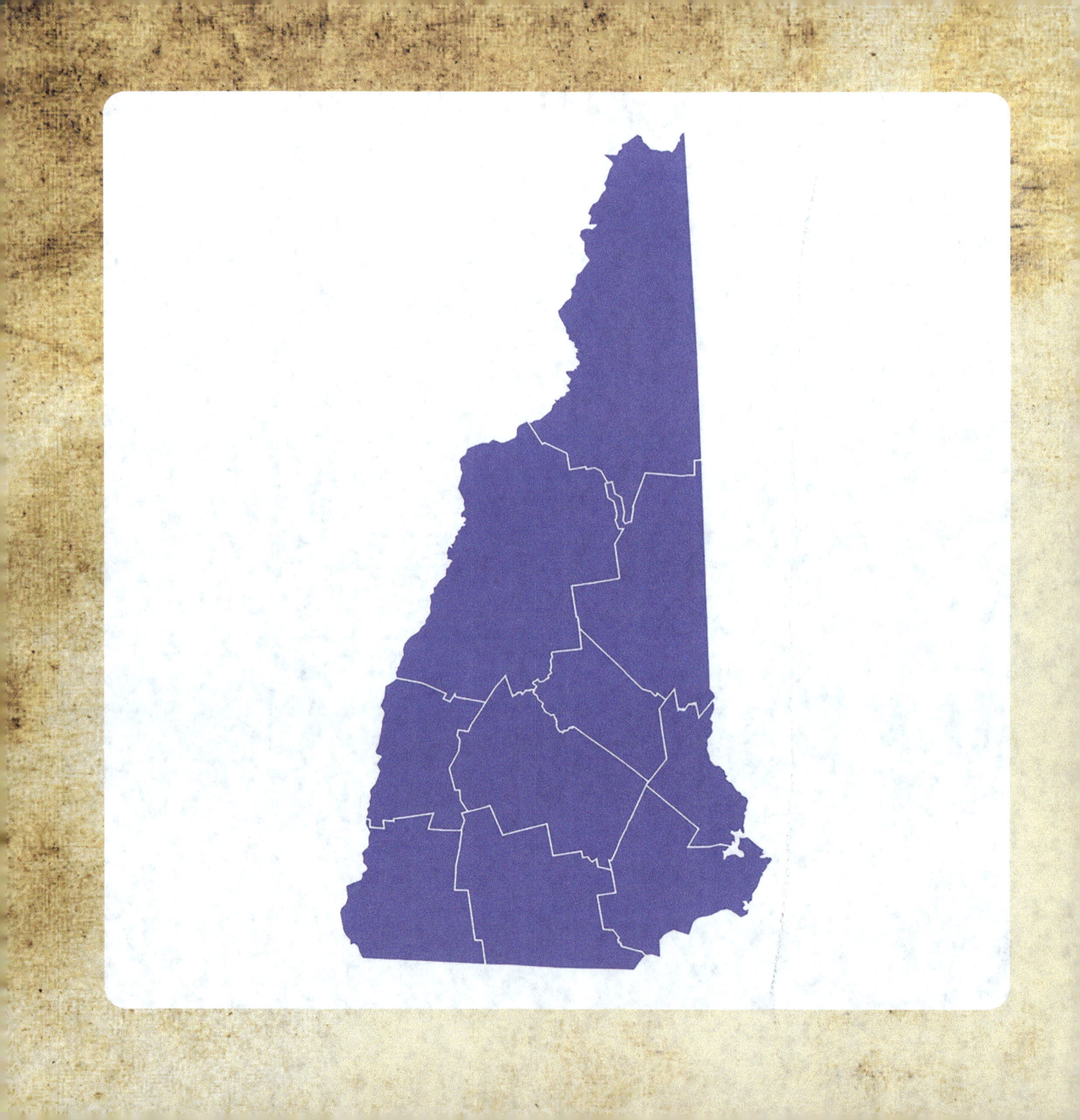

was formally organized as an
English royal colony on
October 7, 1691.
The territory is now the U.S.
state of New Hampshire.

THE PROVINCE OF MASSACHUSETTS BAY

was chartered on October 7, 1691. The name Massachusetts comes from the Massachusett, an Algonquian tribe.

COLONY OF RHODE ISLAND AND PROVIDENCE PLANTATIONS

was established on the east coast of North America. Providence Plantations was an American colony of English settlers founded in 1636 by Roger Williams.

CONNECTICUT COLONY

originally known as the River Colony, it was organized on March 3, 1636. The colony was later the scene of a bloody and raging Pequot War.

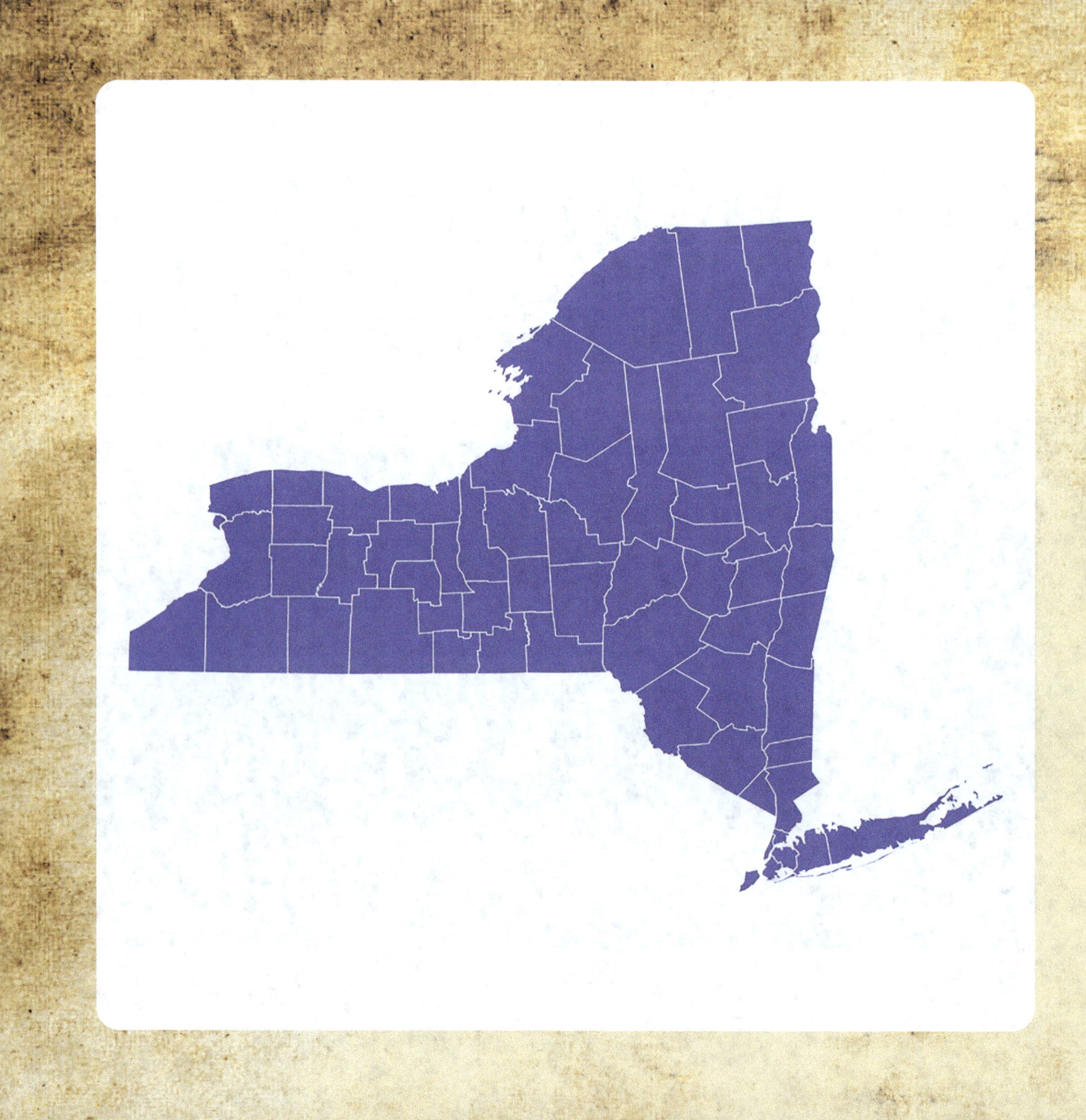

PROVINCE OF NEW YORK

was an English and later British crown territory. The Province of New York was divided into twelve counties on November 1, 1683.

PROVINCE OF NEW JERSEY

was one of the Middle Colonies of Colonial America. The Province of New Jersey was originally settled in the 1610s as part of the colony of New Netherland.

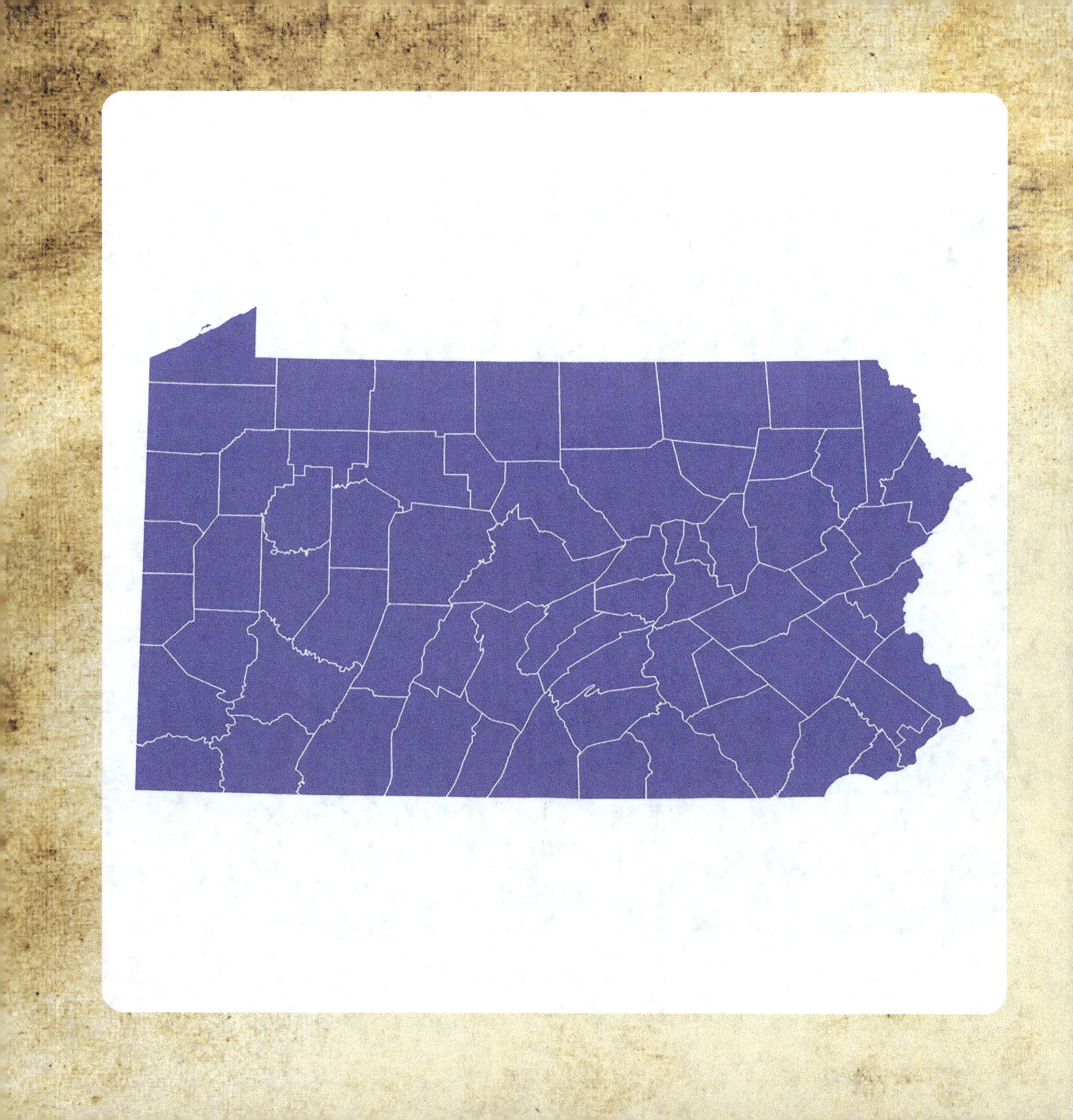

PROVINCE OF PENNSYLVANIA

was founded in English North America on March 4, 1681. The Province of Pennsylvania was one of the two major restoration colonies.

DELAWARE COLONY

was founded in 1638 by Peter Minuit. The Delaware Colony was divided into three counties in 1682 including New Castle, Sussex, and Kent.

PROVINCE OF MARYLAND

was an English and later British colony in North America. The Maryland Colony was founded by Cecil Calvert, Lord Baltimore and others in 1633 at Baltimore.

COLONY AND DOMINION OF VIRGINIA

was the first English colony in the world. The Virginia Colony was founded by John Smith and other colonists in 1607.

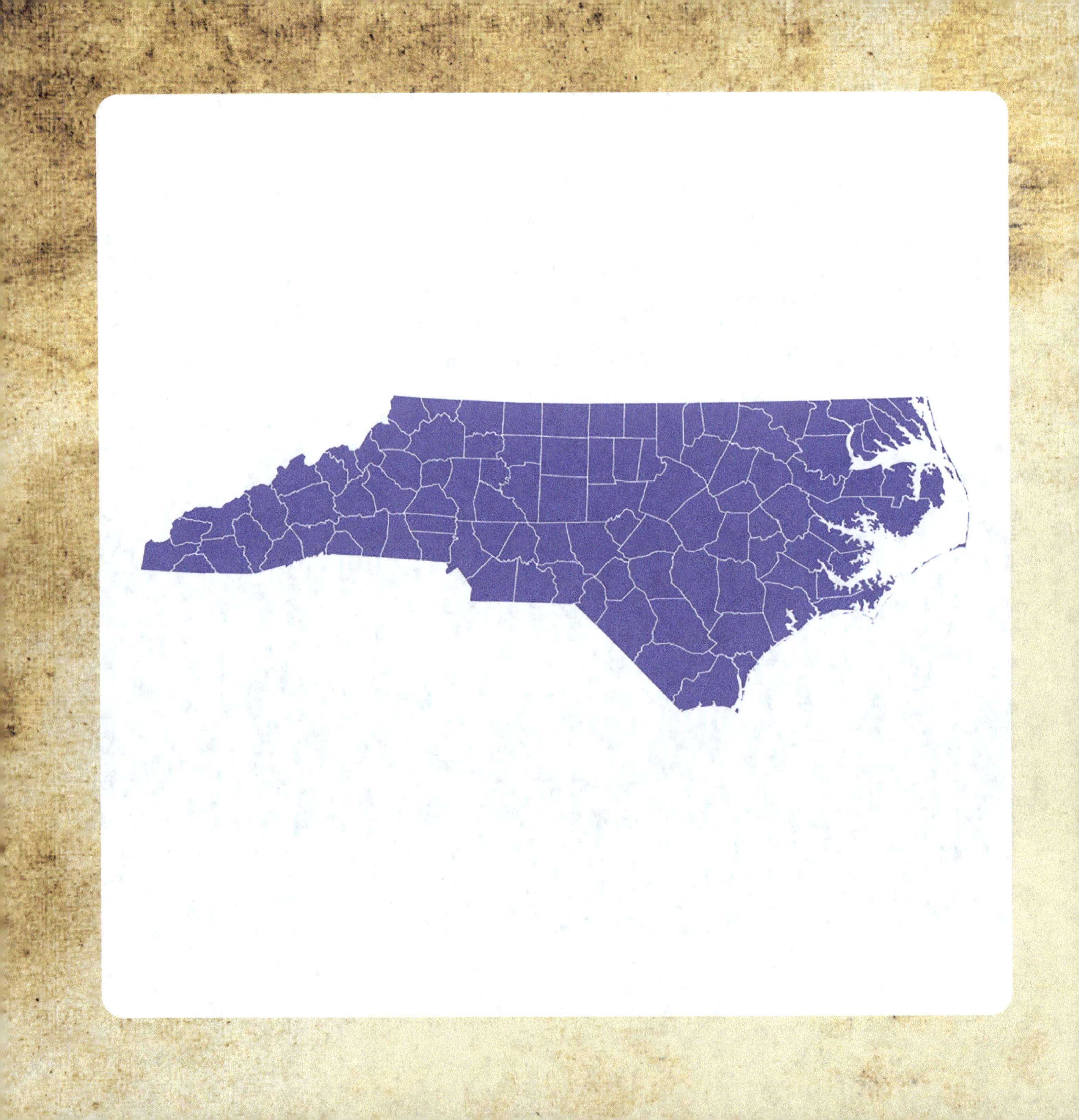

PROVINCE OF NORTH CAROLINA

was founded in 1653. Carolina is a word derived from the Latin name for Charles, 'Carolus'.

PROVINCE OF SOUTH CAROLINA

was founded in 1633 under
the Charter of Carolina. In 1729
the South Carolina Colony
became a royal colony.

PROVINCE OF GEORGIA

was founded in 1732 by several colonists including James Oglethorpe. The Georgia Colony was one of the Southern colonies in British America.

LAKE
UPPER
Montrea I.
Long I.
R. St Louis
Pontchartrain
Royal
12 Apostles
Philippeaux
SUPERIOR
Falls of St Mary
St Mary's R.
OUTAOUACS
Falls of St Anthony
St Peter
St Croix
LAKE HURON
Mississippi R.
Chippeway R.
Vermillion R.
Green Bay
Michilimack
Missilimak Fort
Yellow R.
Rum R.
OUTAGAMIES
Ouisconsin R.
Fox River
LAKE MICHIGAN
UTAWAS
Lake St Clair
Fort St Clair
MASCOUTENS
Rocky R.
St Joseph R.
Detroit
Chicago
LAKE ERIE
Theakiki R.
WESTERN
R. Miami of the Lake
Sandusky
L. Illinois
ILLINOIS
Ft Miami
Ft Recovery
COUNTRY
Kiskushk
Illinois R.
MIAMIES
Ft Jefferson
Gt Miami R.
Muskingum R.
Extensive Meadows
Little Miami R.
TERRITORY
Ohio R.
Gallipolis
R. Missouri
St Louis
Post St Vincent
Ft Hamilton
Washingtonton
Ohio R.
Big Kenhawa R.
Green Briar R.
Rackaby R.
Wabash R.
Rapids
R.
Kentucky R.
Monongahela R.
Mississippi R.
Louisville
Lexington
New Madrid
Iron Banks
Ohio R.
Kentucky
KENTU
Salt
Boonsborough
Lincoln
Danville
Clark Mounts
Alleghany Mountain
Blue Ridge
Green R.
Cumberland R.
LOUISIANA
Red R.
Clarksville
Tenessee R.
Cumberland R.
Nashville
Duck R.
Knoxville
Holston R.
Clinch R.
Laurel
Dan R.
Elk R.
TENESSEE
French Broad R.
Holston R.
Nola Chucky R.
NORTH C
Salisbury
Charlotte
CHICASAWS
CHEROKEES
Ninety Six
Camden
Orangeburg
STH CAROL
Yazous
Tenessee R.
Tuscaloosa R.
Little R.
Santee R.
Windsor
Dorchester
Augusta
George Town
GEORGIA
Chactaws
Pearl R.
Tombigby R.
Alabama R.
Savannah
St Catherins
MUSKOGEES
St Simonds Sd
Natches
Appalachicola Ft
St Marys R.
Amelia I. & Sound
WEST
FLORIDA
Mobile
EAST
FLORIDA
St Georges Fort
St Johns Sd
New Orleans
GULF
OF MEXICO

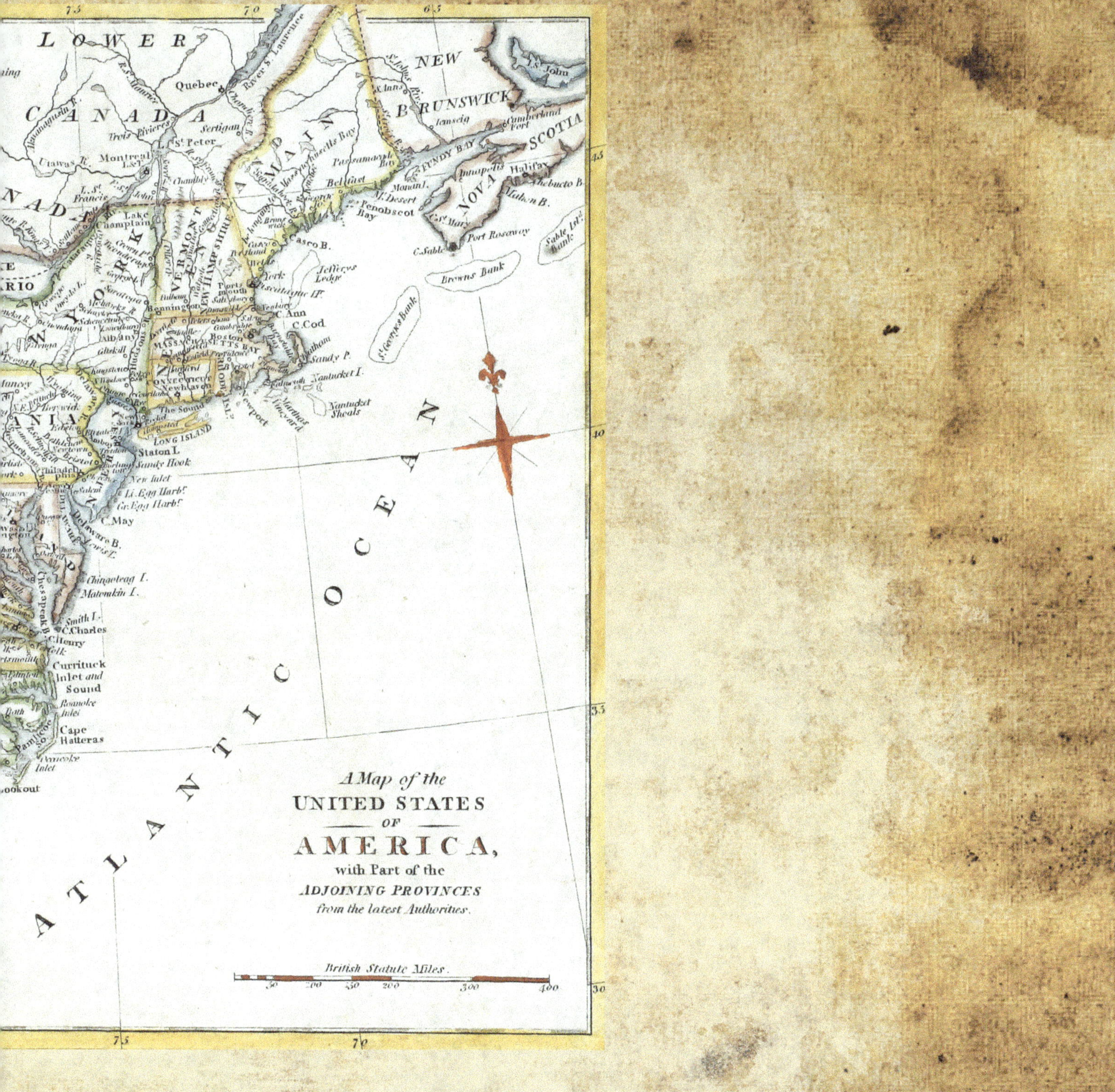

LOWER CANADA
CANADA
NEW BRUNSWICK
NOVA SCOTIA
Quebec
Montreal
Trois Rivieres
Utawas R.
St. Francis
Lake Champlain
MAINE
NEW YORK
VERMONT
NEW HAMPSHIRE
MASSACHUSETTS BAY
CONNECTICUT
Boston
Albany
Saratoga
Bennington
Portsmouth
Newhaven
LONG ISLAND
Staten I.
Sandy Hook
New York
Newport
Nantucket I.
Nantucket Shoals
Casco B.
C. Ann
C. Cod
Massachusetts Bay
Passamaquoddy Bay
Penobscot Bay
Mt. Desert
St. Mary
Port Roseway
C. Sable
Halifax
Chebucto B.
St. Johns River
St. Anns River
FUNDY BAY
Annapolis
Cumberland Fort
I. St. John
Sable Isl. Bank
Browns Bank
St. Georges Bank
Jefferys Ledge
Piscataqua R.
Delaware B.
C. May
Li. Egg Harb.
Gr. Egg Harb.
New Inlet
Chesapeak
Chingoteag I.
Matomkin I.
Smith I.
C. Charles
C. Henry
Currituck Inlet and Sound
Roanoke Inlet
Cape Hatteras
Pamlico
Roanoke Inlet
Lookout
PENNSYLVANIA
MARYLAND
Philadelphia
Bristol
Baltimore
ATLANTIC OCEAN
A Map of the
UNITED STATES
OF
AMERICA,
with Part of the
ADJOINING PROVINCES
from the latest Authorities.
British Statute Miles.
50   100   150   200   300   400
75   70   65   45   40   35   30